Charles Jones

T0087868

FIVE MELODIES

FOR VIOLIN
AND PIANO

ISBN-13: 978-1-4234-1976-1
ISBN-10: 1-4234-1976-6

PIEDMONT MUSIC COMPANY
Administered by Edward B. Marks Music Company
126 East 38th Street
New York, New York 10016

FIVE MELODIES
for Violin and Piano

Charles Jones
(1910–1997)

I. March

Tempo di marcia ♩ = 108

II. Barcarole

III. Scherzo

Violin

FIVE MELODIES
for Violin and Piano

Charles Jones
(1910–1997)

I. March

Violin

Violin

II. Barcarole

Violin

Violin

III. Scherzo

Violin

Violin

IV. Waltz

Violin

V. Finale

Violin

IV. Waltz

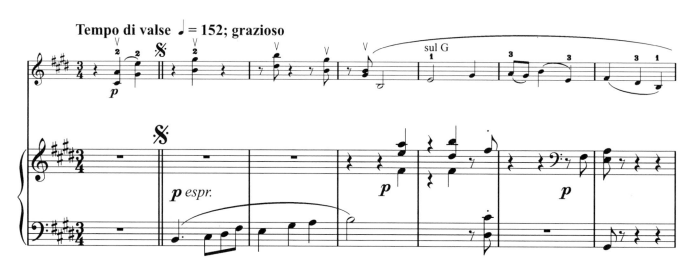

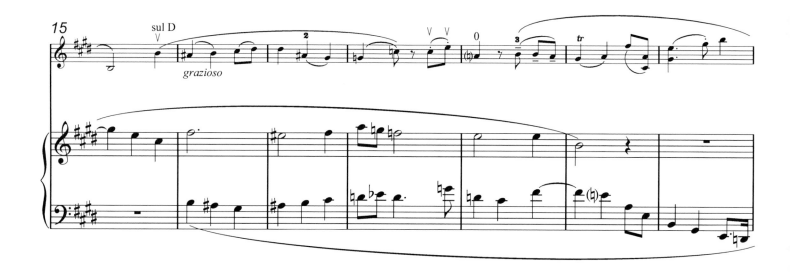

V. Finale

December 19, 1945

BIOGRAPHY

Charles Jones was born in Tamworth, Ontario, Canada on June 21, 1910. At the age of ten he moved to Toronto where he studied the violin and music theory. In 1928 he went to New York City and studied at the Institute of Musical Art with Sascha Jacobson. He graduated in 1932 as a violinist.

In 1935 Jones entered the Juilliard School on a fellowship. He studied composition with Bernard Wagenaar and graduated in 1939. He began teaching at Mills College in California. There he met fellow teacher, the French composer Darius Milhaud. This began both a lifelong friendship and thirty year collegial teaching relationship between the two composers, first at Mills College then at the Music Academy of the West in Santa Barbara, and finally at the Aspen Music Festival in Colorado. Whereas Milhaud retired from teaching in America in 1969, Jones continued at the Aspen Music Festival as composer-in-residence until 1989.

In 1946, Jones and his wife moved from California to New York. He taught at the Juilliard School beginning in 1954, and later at the Mannes College of Music. He also taught briefly at the Salzburg Seminar in Austria and at the Bryanston School in England. He died on June 6, 1997.

Admired and respected as a teacher, Jones composed some ninety works for many combinations, including four symphonies, nine string quartets, numerous vocal scores and many other combinations. His music was performed in his lifetime by the New York Philharmonic; NBC Symphony; Radiodiffusion, Paris; Brussels Festival; ISCM Festival; Aspen Music Festival; National, San Francisco, St. Louis, Dallas, Denver, Toledo, and Duluth Symphonies; Gäble Symphony Orchestra for Swedish Radio; Upsala Chamber Orchestra; Suisse Romande Radio; Canadian Broadcasting Corporation; and the BBC. His music is recorded on the CRI and Albany labels.

A NOTE ABOUT THE COMPOSITION

The *Five Melodies for Violin and Piano* is an adaptation by the composer of his *Five Melodies for Orchestra*. The orchestral work was completed on August 26, 1945 and dedicated to Vladimir Golschmann, and the present suite was completed on December 19 of the same year. In a style not unlike that of one of Jones's strongest influences at the time, Igor Stravinsky, the movements are titled after familiar classical and popular forms – March, Barcarolle, Scherzo, Waltz and Finale. (Interestingly, the Scherzo is called Tarantella in the orchestral work, yet is essentially unchanged musically.) The Suite aptly demonstrates Charles Jones's affinity for and inside knowledge of the violin via its virtuosic use of double- and triple-stops, rolled chords, elaborate harmonics, left hand pizzicati, open string accompaniments, and other devices. All bowings and fingerings in this edition are the composer's. The chamber work goes far beyond being a mere orchestral reduction – rather, in bringing the larger instrumentation into the domain of the present duo, Jones found the perfect vehicle for displaying his skill in composing for the instruments, while remaining at the service of a delightful melodic and harmonic language of his own creation.